M000034692

March, before Spring

The Midi Canal

He sat on the stone ledge, swung his feet
into the water, grinned for the camera like a child
as he tossed bread to the waiting ducks.
Their maps and phrase book couldn't tell them
why he was tired, what the cough was all about.

In a meadow, they came to a stone door frame—
the remains of a wall clung to its sides.
She wouldn't walk through it, afraid she'd jinx
this happiness, took a photo instead,
and they headed back to the barge called *The Quest*.

That night he ordered trout at a restaurant.
In the stocked pond behind the kitchen, the cook
netted the biggest. The wife wondered if the fish
knew why the pond was there.

March, before Spring

STEPHANIE MENDEL

O'BRIEN & WHITAKER

OAKLAND, CALIFORNIA · 1999

—for John

It is only with the heart that one can see rightly;
what is essential is invisible to the eye.

ANTOINE DE SAINT-EXUPÉRY

The Small Deaths

The doctor tells you in a voice not shaking,
You have lung cancer and it's not fixable.
This is the most amazing thing
anyone has ever told us. We ask
a few questions. He answers,

Perhaps six months or less. He doesn't
know about pain. I don't say *thank you*
or even *bye* when we leave. We don't stop
for the new fuse for the rain gauge,
we get into bed and cry.

We tell ourselves we're lucky
it isn't a sudden death, like if
a plane went down. You say,
*If I wear my new suspenders, I want
one side of my jacket to be open.*

Afraid not many people
will come to the funeral,
you suggest door prizes.
I laugh like a teenager—
we're not old enough for this.

Later, I lay my hand on your rib cage,
bargain with the fist-sized cancer,
try to soothe it by telling it
if it grows slowly, it can live longer,
but I know it's too greedy to care.

Learning

Soon our mouths will form words
we're not used to: *metastasized,*
palliative, hospice, morphine.
In five months I'll learn how
to spell *deceased.*

The Path

In the waiting room I feel an odd kind
of success as I fit in the last border piece
of the jigsaw puzzle. I'm impatient
to return tomorrow and start on the face
of the lioness, those piercing eyes—
maybe she'll tell me how to save you.
If I can just convince you to eat my custards
maybe the cancer will go into remission.
In the room where they shoot radiation
into your chest, you stare at the poster
of Monet's garden on the ceiling, say
you have found a path among the trees.

Halloween

I've memorized the number for hospice.
Friends call and you answer with hellos
that mean good-bye.

Snow White and Darth Vader,
a peacock in rain boots seem more real
than the chest X-ray at the doctor's office,

but I make a note to have the lock
on the sliding door fixed, wonder how
to change the cartridge in the printer.

Soon I'll write an obituary,
place photographs in your suit pocket,
choose a casket. You said, *Get a king-sized one.*

Your Last Birthday

No more four-mile walks on the bike path,
then not even a stroll to breathe
the star jasmine in the front yard.
Too soon you couldn't walk downstairs,
or get to the chair beside the bed.

You slept more, ate less, scolded me
for force-feeding you like a goose,
said losing weight would make
the casket lighter, easier to carry.
I didn't think this was funny.

Doug made pasta for your birthday,
wore your chef's hat, your walking shoes.
I made a birthday cake, your mother's recipe.
Like a child, you asked if you could
have your cake before your salad—
but wanted no candles, made no wish.

I gave you yellow and white striped pajamas,
which you wore for visitors and sometimes for me.
You wanted to grow a beard. I asked death
to hold off until the gray stubble grew
to a generous shape.

In the Last Month

Doug visits, asks you
if he can do CPR if you stop breathing.
He says *if*, not *when*,
walks out the door three times
before he drives away.

Now

A tile in the kitchen floor cracks.
That means they all can crack.
The winds are driving me crazy.
I try to sleep downstairs,
but want to be with you.

A month ago you ate Brie
and Häagen Dazs. Now the tumor
strangles your appetite.

You're called for jury duty.
The doctor writes a note
excusing you for two years.
I don't get that, but I'm watching
life through glasses
with the wrong prescription.

The nurse leaves a message
on the answering machine:
Elevate leg and apply heat.
You hear, *Elevate leg five feet.*
We still laugh.

The kids come with Indian food,
but a milkshake for you.
You watch us eat picnic-style
on the bedroom floor.

I type up the correct spelling
of each medication, alphabetize them,
say what each is for, believe
this may save you,

but when mail comes,
I throw out the Macy's catalog
showing suits and men's cologne.

The nurse talks about a hospital bed.
No, you say, *I need my wife to sleep with me.*
Do you know how scared you sound?

You tell me you're beginning
to understand I'll be alone after you die.
I may stick around, you say.
When you hear noises at night, it's me.

You complain that eating
will make you live longer.
I hope food will buy me time.

I can't trust your judgment now,
keep pills where you can't reach them.

You say there's too much milk
in the kugel, that I put the wastebasket
where you can't reach it. You say
my hands are too cold.

The Arrival

Your back is tanned a bronze
you'd see in a fashion magazine.
The radiation treatments.

There's nothing more
the doctor can do.
The house seems to shiver

as the hospital bed arrives.
Wind thrashes at the oak tree.
Only one half survives.

Swallowing

I tell you you only have two pills
to take tonight. *You're harassing me,*
you say in a hoarse whisper. *That's like saying*
I only have to swallow two elephant eggs!

The Pen

Renew driver's license
had long ago been taken off the list.
Now you weren't even a passenger—
the doctor came to you.

You told David how to clean out
the drain spouts, oil the furnace.
Your calendar stayed in a drawer.
Your pen rolled behind the bed table
and wasn't missed.

I would offer you applesauce,
ice cream, matzo. Gradually
you stopped eating, accepted Gatorade
only to get pills down. Soon, you couldn't
form words, turn over, sip water.

Bridges

Pound by pound you slip away.
I hope the ficus is considerate—
waits to lose its leaves until you die.

You won't get out of bed again.
Shoes rest in the closet,
the walker's stored away.

We're not brave, but move
from bridge to bridge, and won't fall in.
Only our son's old stuffed bear
with corduroy paws sits against
the wall, stunned.

Preparing

Last week you could still talk,
told me not to sit on a suitcase
that wasn't there at the end of the bed.
You slept between breaths
and my breath would stop
as I waited for your chest to rise again,
my hand holding yours, claiming
what was still mine.

Your fingers, in spasm, gripped mine,
and I was determined
to soften those final days,
bathed you with a warm washcloth,
brought you heavier socks—
your feet already so cold.
I fed you water through a dropper,
adjusted the shutters
to the darkness you now preferred.

Was I crazy, feeling I had so much—
our palms pressed together,
your heart still beating?
You groaned as I left the room for
more morphine—I didn't know
you could still respond!
Like when we dated, I felt so lucky.
For that moment, I forgot that
you were practicing touch-and-go's,
the wheels of the plane barely
touching down, as you prepared to solo.

March, before Spring

When your heart stopped beating
my hand was resting on your chest.
While loss and courage struggled
to find a meeting place, I had to
phone hospice, the rabbi, wake the boys.
Were they *our sons* or *my sons* now?
Do I tell people I *love* you or I *loved* you?
Do I stop wearing my wedding ring?

Three times I closed your eyes,
three times they opened again.
This made sense to me, even in death.
David brought me a cup of orange spice tea,
Doug read you the letter he would read
at the cemetery. I hoped the hospice nurse
would lose her way, not come to write in
the time of death, call the mortuary.

Months ago, you had flung some
of my bras onto the tall ficus
in the bedroom and hid the rest.
When I take out my black purse for
the funeral, I'll find them, and a jade ring
like the one that broke, and a note:
See if United can fly you up to visit me.

The Moment

I had expected death to have
a Jack Nicholson laugh, the moment
to be startling like the green flash
when the sun disappears. Instead,
there was quiet.

Journey

The bathroom shelf, chaotic.
Bottles, patches, syringes,
swabs, tubes of creams.
Forty-three items. More
in the refrigerator. *Take at night,*
with meals, once every 4 hours,
once a day, only when needed.

Keeping your sense of humor,
you said, *Triamcinolone must be*
for masturbation, not dry skin.

Your long bony frame barely fits
into the body bag. *Be careful,*
I tell the men. Come close
to adding, *he has a bad back.*
A man carries your suit
with the two photographs
in the breast pocket. I left
a Berkeley Rep ticket stub
in the pocket of your pants.
The long car drives you away.
It's like watching a movie
I don't understand.

Insisting

My body had protested,
I can't do this anymore,
and I had insisted, *Find a way!*

And when your death came
I forgave the weariness
for feeling relieved.

Playing Games

You loved to surprise me.
Like that day you met me at the door,
asked me to keep my eyes closed,
to crawl in the dark. I found myself
in a tent, the price tag still on.

The living room floor was hard,
the sex funny. The next day
you went back for sleeping bags,
a list of campgrounds.

Why shouldn't you still surprise me?
Yesterday, under the ceiling fan,
sweating in a camisole and shorts,
I found a paper snowflake—
it had to be from you.

Your watch slid almost up to your elbow
that last month, and even now
still beats out the seconds—
don't you think it's time to give up
this game of playing dead?

Misery

Its chill woke me at three A.M.
A whole day to get through.
I forget to eat the defrosted bagel,
and simple things go on happening—
the hum of cars, a dog barking.
Everyone has something to do.
When you were dying, you said,
Noon to midnight is the hardest time.
Want to know the second hardest?
I wish for anything I don't have.

In Shadow

A boy at the house across the lagoon,
inspecting his rowboat. His silhouette tall,
shoulders wide, hands loose on hips.
Two buddies with beer, laughing,
voices fast, the three untying the boat,
jumping in, splashing, laughing harder,
getting the feel for oars and direction,
their sound echoing over the water.
They don't see me sitting under a willow,
not knowing how to do what they do so easily.

Before and After

It was so simple.
You'd come down the aisle
with a tub of popcorn and a Pepsi.
I'd reach for them so you could find space
for your long legs, take off your jacket.
You'd hold the popcorn between your knees,
your hand would reach for mine.
It was a time to make plans:
The farmers' market—who'd wait
in line for coffee, who for bread?
Should we pick up ribs on the way home?
The lights would go out
and your arm would be around me.

Now I pick a seat toward the back
between two empty ones,
not close to the front where we used to sit.
The theater is full. A man sits down
next to me. I divide my attention
between the movie and leaning away from him.
On screen Jim Lovell makes his way home
from an ill-fated mission to the moon.
His wife waits for him.
I take Kleenex from my pocket, careful
not to brush against the man next to me.
That's when I almost walk out,
but I want to pass this test.

The Call

The operator asks if I'd accept
a collect call from John Mendel.
I don't have the words to answer her.
She's impatient, asks if I know
a John Mendel. He was my husband,
I say. He died last month.
Her voice is soft as she apologizes.
The call unnerves me. A crank?
But you didn't always accept
the limits other people did. I tell you
to use Doug's name next time—
that way for sure you'll get through.

The Trip to Napa

You would have liked the drive.
I played Jimmy Buffett. You know,
"My head hurts, my feet stink,
and I don't love Jesus . . ."
I tried singing along, but ended up howling—
you wouldn't have known me.
I quieted down only at the stoplight
and didn't get lost, even coming home
when lefts became rights, and the scenery
changed like when we went counterclockwise
around the pond on Orcas Island.

The Culinary Institute was where
Christian Brothers used to be
and I wasn't ready for that,
but our tree-lined roads and
the Oakville Grocery were still there
and it was near ninety, like the day
we picnicked in the car behind the market
and I dropped the pickles on the seat
and when we went in for paper towels
you lost your keys and I had to pee quick
before I could look for them.

I was always the one who'd find things
but since you died,
at daybreak, before my eyes open,
my body shifts to your side of the bed
and every morning brings the same surprise.

Time Out

I'm taking the day off
from knowing you're dead.
I don't believe in logic
and look for you on the bike path.

At home, a puffball of dandelion seeds
floats over to me. It stays a moment
before the wind carries it over the fence.
It's important to me not to catch it,
but one white strand sticks to my jeans.
I place it on a green marble tray,
away from drafts.

When I lie down, I hear you
say *hi* as you come up the stairs.
As I drift off to sleep, I hear you moan—
the sound coming from a place
near my pillow.

Evidence

It isn't your nature to waste anything,
and there are maybe two hundred
business cards still in your drawer.

In the dark I reach for you, but maybe
you're at the desk figuring out what to do
with the frequent flyer miles
that expire in April.

There are recipes you've marked "cook soon"—
shrimp with papaya, the orange soufflé,
and there's a pint of your chicken stock
left in the freezer.

You've only been scuba diving once,
and the prescription goggles
were ridiculously expensive, which goes to prove
that you can't be dead.

Widow

I keep pruners by the door
to cut flowers for your grave,
in your car a straw hat, a folding chair.
I find the missing *Books on Tape,*
a French franc under the driver's seat.

I wear your T-shirts to bed,
your shirts with my jeans.
I avoid the dining room,
eat dinner standing at the sink.

I give away your size 13 ski boots,
your left-handed scissors, cling
to the idea that you believe in me
as I learn to relight the pilot,
drive alone at night.

I'm confused when your presence
seems to leave and return at will,
want to learn to manage grief
as easily as I peel this pear.

The Visit

I wasn't sure you were there
when I placed daffodils on your grave.
Your photo in the kitchen had darkened
when I told you I'd be at Sea Ranch for a week
so maybe you were still visiting the house.
I run my fingers over your lips in the photo.
You catch the side of a finger in your mouth.
How much longer will this happen?
Like a Polaroid in reverse, will you
disappear altogether if I miss you any less?

What the Dead Know

I check my lipstick in the car mirror, Fiery Rose.
Then step out onto the grass, walk over
to the headstone. It's our anniversary,

a day unlike that afternoon at Union Square,
when you walked toward me grinning,
holding roses from a street vendor.

I want to do something for you,
clear the grass of eucalyptus leaves,
the stems of the sunflowers I brought last week.
I'd hoped the deer wouldn't get them—
I often wish for the impossible.

One of the kids' old camp blankets protects me
from grass stains as I rest against
the coolness of the double stone.

I tell you the pelicans are back,
that the banana trees are taller than ever,
that the boys will be at the house
for your 60th birthday.

You give no sign that you know I'm here.

It isn't until I get home and see your photo
on the table that your eyes tell me
the dead know what they're missing,
and it hurts too much to talk about it.

Thirty-fifth Reunion

I'll be at your grave
when the service starts
for those of you who have died
since graduation. It was my life too—

What We Tell Each Other

A large bird glides over the cemetery.
I have sunflowers for you, and read
you David and Holly's postcard from Egypt.
I tell you Doug rented a U-Haul, moved
even the windsurfer to his cabin. I ask
if you can come by to smell the tomatoes—
know I should have brought one with me.
I tell you the bamboo is coming up through
the cement in Mildred's garage. I thought
you'd be interested, but can tell you're impatient
and are waiting for me to simply lie down
next to you, so I do, and it feels good,
the way it always has.

The Son

David says I can stay here all day,
shows me which bread is freshest.
I read *The Frugal Gourmet* on the sofa
that used to be in our family room.
Outside an owl hoots, and I hear
the steady clipping of shears,
slowly realize it's a clock somewhere
in this spacious house. I like not knowing
where it is, that I'm not responsible
for its accuracy. Last night when
I turned on the VCR, David watched me
as I listened to "Dueling Banjos,"
showed me the button to push for replay
so I could stay with the sweetness,
not go on to the brutal deaths.

Passage

Suppose I moved your photo
from the bedroom into the hall—
would your eyes still be patient as I

hurried past you to answer the phone,
start the washer, rush out the door?

Suppose I wore my wedding ring
on my right hand? Would the nakedness
shame me, make me too available?

Suppose I liked the sound of his voice,
the way he kissed my shoulder?

Suppose I were walking on a bridge
that began to sway too much and I ran
to the other side instead of heading back.

My grateful acknowledgment to the editors of the following publications in which some of these poems first appeared, some of them in different forms: *33 Review, Barnabe Mountain Review, Marin Poetry Center Anthology, Poet Lore,* and *Rattle.*

My deep appreciation to Patricia Edith, Peter Harris-Kunz, Sharon Fain, Dorianne Laux, Dale Going, Robin Jacobson, Jaime Robles, Marian O'Brien and Keith Whitaker for their nurturing patience and generosity of time.

Copyright © 1999 by Stephanie Mendel

Designed by Jaime Robles and Stephanie Mendel, using Sabon type with Cezanne initial caps. Printed by West Coast Print Center on Starwhite Vicksburg Archiva. Cover photograph by the author.

ISBN 0-9668431-1-8

O'Brien & Whitaker Publishers
Oakland, California
510.663.7061 or books@obandw.com

March, before Spring is available through Small Press Distribution
800.869.7553 or 510.524.1668
and orders@spdbooks.org

Stephanie Mendel is from Pittsburgh, Pennsylvania, and has lived in the San Francisco Bay Area for thirty-six years. She and her late husband met in Ann Arbor, Michigan, and were married in 1959. They have two grown sons and a grandson. Stephanie teaches writing privately, and her work has appeared in journals including *Barnabe Mountain Review, The Cream City Review* and *Poet Lore,* as well as *The Saturday Evening Post, The Western Journal of Medicine* and *The Poet's Companion,* published by Norton in 1997.